AMERICAN BUG

American Bug

ISBN
Paperback: 978-0-578-25180-6
Hardcover: 978-0-578-25187-5
E-book: 978-0-578-25188-2

Printed in the United States of America.

Cover artwork by Jorge Santiago, Jr.
Book design by Jorge Santiago, Jr.
Illustration on page 23 by Richard Pace
Illustration on page 47 by Kevin P. West
Short essay on pages 24-25 by Joseph Duis

10 9 8 7 6 5 4 3 2 1

This one’s for you, the reader.

Because we’re all in this together.

Preface

"All you forgotten in the projects, I hear ya
All you numbers in the cell block, we care
All you sweatin' in the detox, we care
To all you hoods that are dodging cops, we care
To all you bleeding from a broken heart, you know you've got a brother here
You've got a brother here!"
-Blood for Blood, 2004, Victory Records

The night started off hopeful on November 8th, 2016. All the polls projected Hillary Clinton as the winner of the United States presidential election. Both NPR and Five-Thirty-Eight reported the possibility of a Trump victory. However, all the analysists still predicted little to no chance of Trump winning. But then, it happened. I saw on the screen that more and more states were going red. The swing states of North Carolina and Florida voted for Trump. And by the end of the night, the blue states of Michigan, Pennsylvania and Wisconsin voted for Trump as well.

As the night progressed, I had a sinking feeling. My throat felt like it was closing, and my head was spinning. My chest felt extremely heavy. I was in shock and disbelief. I remember Trevor Noah and Roy Wood Junior quipping on the Daily Show about how terrified they were about what might happen. I felt it, too. It was a paralyzing fear. It looked a pathological liar and a reality TV star who over a dozen women accused of sexual assault really might become the president of the United States.

Since that night, everything has changed. The world has changed. The country has changed. Political discourse has changed. And I, most certainly, have changed. Something within me woke up from hibernation. It wasn't anything new. In fact, it was something inside of me that had been there for a long time. It was a fire that never burnt out and yet, over time, I'd almost forgotten it was there. It was the same fire that compelled me to tag an anarchy sign on an underpass when I was 16 years old. It was the same fire that compelled me to write poems like "Room

Number Zero" and "Cataclysmic" in my first book of poetry, "As the Moonlight Shines". It was the same fire that after the killing of George Floyd brought millions to the streets in all fifty states and every continent except Antarctica.

To be clear, *American Bug* is an entirely different project than my first book of poetry, *As the Moonlight Shines*. While that book did have some social commentary, it wasn't the mission statement. *As the Moonlight Shines* was about grief and loss. It was mostly written during a period of my life when I was coping with the death of a dear friend. In other words, *As the Moonlight Shines* was a product of my own introspection. In *American Bug*, I have completely shifted the focus from looking inside of me to observing the world around me. While *American Bug* is certainly about me, it's also about the people I know and love. It's about the power-hungry and the corrupt who piss me off. It's about my fellow underdogs with whom I want to express solidarity. And finally, it's about my own experiences as a millennial writer and why comics broke my heart.

This book is a product of the Trump era, but it's about so much more. It's about a woman with a side hustle who is doing what she can to take care of her disabled grandma. It's about a warehouse employee who is worried he may be fired soon for not working fast enough. It's about you. It's about me. It's about us. It's about the American bugs and the workers of the world. Because even with Trump out of the White House today, we're still living under global capitalism. That hasn't changed in the least.

So, pour yourself a late-night cup of coffee, get settled into a comfortable chair and read the poems in this collection. I hope they make you laugh. I hope they make you cry. And I hope they cause you to pause and reflect. But please don't let the stories and imagery on these pages sadden you. Let them radicalize you.

Nick Ulanowski

Chicago, Illinois

March 16th, 2021

Foreword

The time before and after the 2016 election feel like two different eras: the unimaginable lead-up, a joke that turned into an awful, awful horror film, and then the gruesome aftermath. Fascism fattened and festered in America's skin, and the boil still hasn't popped. It's swelling, reddening, filling with the puss of QAnon, red pills, and bloody, blue lines, and Jesus, does it need a lancing. I'd apologize for the gross metaphor but it's a gross society.

I truly believe everyone feels how gross it is, subconsciously. It's natural to want to look away. There's a shame we live with, as parents, aunts and uncles, sisters and brothers, friends and coworkers, neighbors, and that old man who waved from across the street take to Facebook and vomit all over the page. It's sick. We're sick.

Over the years with my friend Nick Ulanowski, much of our conversations have revolved around our mutual… disgust? Despair? Powerlessness?... all of the above, really, in regards to current events. It'd always been there, Nick would tell me, and Trump was just the latest incarnation. He didn't start it. He's a symptom. We'd been gross a long time.

Eventually, I stopped checking news sites. I unsubscribed from my usual current events YouTubers. I stopped watching politics to the point where the almighty YouTube algorithm finally gave up and now pretty much sticks to recommending cute animal videos (a win whichever way you want to spin it). I stepped back from most of my social media accounts, and I would later delete them altogether when the pandemic hit.

At one point in *Winnie the Pooh*, Eeyore's house gets swept away in a flood and he's just kinda fine with it. That was about where I was. I barely had enough energy to spare to make it from the beginning of the day to the end. When Nick brought up current events, we'd talk for a bit then I would say something like, "This is really bumming me out. Let's talk about something else." And we would.

Nick is an author and a journalist, and I could spend this foreword listing his boring credentials and various social justice causes, but what you should really know about Nick is that he's an all-around decent human being who gives a shit about other people. What you should know is that the more often I cut myself off from the news because I couldn't look at that pus-filled boil anymore, the more Nick got involved.

While I checked out, Nick just kept on picking at it. He protested, he rallied, he shared stories of voices who needed to be heard, he knew every gritty detail of whatever new shitshow was raining down at any given moment, and he even (and I shudder to think of it) called out the lunatics on Twitter.

And somewhere along the way, somehow, Nick found optimism.

Ultimately, that's what Nick offers with *American Bug*: desperately needed optimism. It's safe to say they are not poems that look away. They lance the boil open to get a good, pungent whiff of the stank as it oozes out. But afterward it feels a bit cleaner. A bit more able to heal.

American Bug is not about Trumpism, no, but it's a telling backdrop for a generation of hopelessness. It holds a giant, red arrow to the human condition that is surviving as a member of the working poor and asks, "What the fuck? Why the fuck?" And more so, it demonstrates the point of it all. No one has the privilege to look away. It's up to each of us to inspire ourselves to become better than we were yesterday. We have to look. We have to feel. We have to do.

Nick writes that comics will break your heart but here's the thing, he still reads comics. That's all of us. That's *American Bug*.

Deirdre Roberts

Park Forest, Illinois

April 22nd, 2021

P.S. No, Nick, I still haven't watched *Trick 'R Treat*.

Table of Contents

AMERICAN BUG

Nick Ulanowski

Power Dynamics?

Don't mind me, I'm just doing what's right
I got to fight the system and take a stand tonight
So, I'm spittin' on his face
I'm spittin' on his face
Spittin' on a Walmart cashier's face
I'm spittin' on his face
I'm spittin' on his face
I'm spittin' on his face to stick it to capitalism

This Poem Kills Fascists

Beto O'Rourke used to skateboard and he loves to fucking swear
He yells "fuck Trump" with his middle finger in the air
Then he accepts money from the pharmaceutical industry
He tells you to "ride free" like a blood-sucking flea
He's a poseur-ass sell out, endorsing Biden like the rest
He united against Sanders like an establishment pest
But when I turn on cable news, I hear what the pundits say
They say Beto's like me, living a counter-culture way
Well, I'd hate to break it to you but that ain't right
I can tell you about all the fight and it's nothing Beto did tonight
I heard a journo once say Beto flashed a punk rock smile
It was some of the cringiest shit I had heard in quite a while

I got that punk rock smile telling you to smash the state
I got that punk rock smile that says, "it's time to liberate"
With my punk rock smile, I can stay focused and on track
'Cuz without a punk rock smile, the bourgeoisie reigns without pushback

Punk rock means you do it yourself
You make your own music, you don't care about wealth
Big record labels be damned, you sing it loud and proud
Fuck society's rules, we yell, our music's underground
It's inherently radical to say we don't need the capitalist class

We can make great art ourselves without kissing corporate ass

While some may say punk rock isn't meant to be political

They may even claim it's reactionary or to these values diametrical

These people either missed the point or they actively ignored it

When we yelled "fuck authority," we meant "fire your boss"

When we said "fuck the system," we meant "fuck your profit loss"

We fight all of our rulers at whatever the cost

"Woah woah, smash the state

Woah woah, liberate

Woah woah, stay on track

Woah woah, push back!"

I got that punk rock smile telling you to smash the state

I got that punk rock smile that says, "it's time to liberate"

I look you in the eyes and I dare you to defile

Tonight we rise above so put on a punk rock smile

Chest Puffed Out

Creeping slowly down the street in your brand-new Ford
You're on high alert but at the same time bored
It's just another day of looking for trouble on the street
Keep your arrest numbers high, you don't want to be beat
You're the best at what you do and you don't want to cheat
Planting guns, drugs and evidence just ain't your style
That's like hailing a cab and lying, claiming you ran a mile

With a gun strapped to your side, you're looking for a fight
You got your chest puffed out and your badge on tight
It says, "let's show these fuckers who's boss if these bitches want to roll"
Throw 'em on the ground if they resist and break their heart and soul
This is our fucking town, you say, these thugs better recognize
You can send 'em to the reaper so they better stay wise

I don't have to watch a video to know why I feel fear
Your body language says it all with a message loud and clear:
"Stay out of our way when you see us coming through
You better show us some respect 'cuz we're the boys in blue"

I'm a Big Fan of Twiztid

Nosferatu was my nickname and rapping was my game
Spitting that wicked shit with my homie, seeking underground fame
We were just two broke Juggalos making songs for fans on MySpace
Recording in the basement, using beats made at my friend's place
Tetrodotoxin was our name but we called ourselves "TTX" for short
It had something to do with zombies, I don't know, it was my friend's idea of sorts
So, if you're wondering about the "Nosferatu" references in As the Moonlight Shines
This is why they're there, it was my rap name, that's the deeper meaning behind the lines
Me and my homie wrote songs like "4R Juggalos," "Endeavor" and "Sacred Desecration"
We spit lyrics like "you're just a memory" and something about global annihilation
We rapped about werewolves, ghosts and vampires, suicide, murder and hell fires
We called ourselves "horrorcore" and we were influenced by ICP and Twiztid
"Twiztid is the shit," we said, and we also gave the Clowns respect
But that was our moniker to the other Juggalos, we were big fans of Twiztid
And I must admit that to this day, I'm still a big fan of Twiztid

I'm a big fan of Twiztid, I just thought that you should know
I'm a big fan of Twiztid, without them, I wouldn't glow
I'm a big fan of Twiztid, they inspire me to write the things I write
I'm a big fan of Twiztid, like the songs "Nosferatu" and "I'm Alright"

I'm guessing by now you've figured out that I'm kind of a fan of Twiztid
They were referenced in my book Diesel Doctrine - just in case you missed it

In Chapter 5, Mitch says "it's like a Twiztid song and not necessarily reality"
This was on page 29 so if you own the book, go and look and see
I also referenced Twiztid in my book of poetry As the Moonlight Shines
In "Born with a Cigarette in Her Mouth," they're mentioned in the fifteenth line
On page 58, I wrote that I was "puffing on a Port and listening to Twiztid"
This was referring to Newport cigarettes, the same kind smoked by Jamie Madrox
He's one of the members of Twiztid (for those of you who didn't know)
Like I said, I'm a big fan of Twiztid and without them I wouldn't glow

Whenever I hear a Twiztid song, it makes me think about old times
Hanging with my rhyme and crime partner, spitting raps and smoking kind
I can feel and taste the memories as if they were happening right now
Overwhelmed by the darkness I once felt and the balance in the Tao
Even if the grotesque imagery in their lyrics is more than some allow

I'm a big fan of Twiztid, that's why I like to rip them off
I'm a big fan of Twiztid, their ideas are like a contagious cough
I'm a big fan of Twiztid and I call myself a "freak of the night"
I'm a big fan of Twiztid, so DON'T SUE ME, BRO, it wouldn't be polite

Neuro-divergent

A member of society
An individual's anxiety
You can't let them in
but no one will win

Looking for a muting,
a silence of the lambs,
as seventeen bullets
riddle my hand

A twitch of the eye
Rain falls from the sky
These words fly off the mouth
An angry reply

Throwing a fit
A bomb-building kit
But it's all in your head
with a tick-tick-tick

Play your cards right
A roll of the dice
The gamble of life

Refuse to show fright

Belong to a group
Fit in with a clique
or fade into the backdrop
and keep your lips zipped

Comics Will Break Your Heart

With an Illustration by Richard Pace

"Do you have a problem with me?" I asked, like a hot-headed fool
That probably shouldn't have been the first thing I said, it wasn't cool
But I'd been bottling it up for months, tossing and turning in bed
I couldn't understand why you didn't stick up for me, so I was seeing red
I didn't know if it was because you disliked me now or if you just didn't care
I'm sorry I didn't even say "hello," I just burst out and asked you there
It was a complete lack of tact, I was rude, and to my credibility it was a blow
Like, maybe the lies you heard were true and I'm just a low-life zero
Asking you in Artist Alley "is there a problem?" like a crazy weirdo
I'm glad you engaged maturely and we had a heartful, meaningful conversation
To your credit, a different person would have made that a shittier situation

Comics will break your heart, kid
They'll break your stupid heart
Don't read sequential art, stick to reading prose
Because comics will break your heart, kid
Comics will break your heart

You said that wasn't it at all and you were still cool with me
But when I told people you were my friend, it put a target on your head
You said when I dropped your name in my report, it was "like a conflict of interest"
I was reporting a horror comic writer who physically threatened me

I wanted to be able to walk the convention without feeling sick to my stomach
I didn't want to have to worry about him approaching me and flexing his muscles, ick
This writer had intimidated me in Artist Alley and boasted security would take his side
"Who are they gonna believe? Me or you?" he proclaimed, my guts tearing up inside
It turned out he was right because the showrunner banned me from the con instead
I reported a powerful figure for what he did and he was able to get me removed instead
Allowing him to continue his behavior as a predator with fake-ass good-guy cred

Comics will break your heart, kid
Comics will break your heart
Don't let this be your passion, don't go to shows
They'll only break your heart, kid
They'll break your fucking heart

Their harassment policy on the convention's website explicitly mentions "false accusations"
I guess this applied to me, it was fucking bullshit and felt like total devastation
So, I posted online what the horror comic writer did and how the convention handled it
And how the con accused me of lying and how they banned me as if I were the troublemaker
When I said this horror comic writer made me feel afraid, I really truly meant it
But I guess in this process I made an enemy of a showrunner, what the shit?
To your wholehearted credit, you told me you cut your ties with this horror comic writer
But that wasn't because of me but because of others he used and abused
It sounds like you didn't care about me and I'm not sure we were ever really friends
You said me telling people you were my friend was "like a conflict of interest"
You said I went up against a showrunner who runs a con where you make money
But I wasn't trying to attack the showrunner, I just wanted to be able to feel safe

Comics will break your heart, kid

They’ll break your fragile heart

But you can’t let it get to you, you have to just move on

Comics will break your heart, kid

People will break your heart

"Kid, you're one of the best. But put your work in galleries. Don't do comics. Comics will break your heart."

-Jack Kirby

"I'm not sure what exactly Jack Kirby meant when he said, "comics will break your heart, kid." I only know what it's come to mean, which is many things.

It doesn't just mean that you should never meet your heroes.

It doesn't just mean that you spend a lot of money to make comics and aren't likely to have much of a return on investment.

It doesn't just mean that if you follow the same corporate IPs for a long time, you'll eventually give up on them because they're never quite the same as when you started with them.

It doesn't just mean that there's a toxic, authoritarian, bigoted subculture inside of comics that sustains itself through blood money.

It also means that when you make comics, it often feels like you're shouting into the void, and that's the toughest part. It's disheartening to know that the chances are that very few people are ever going to read them. Don't get me wrong. I love it when anyone reads any of our comics. I have a need to make them, and I can't keep doing that if no one buys them and reads them. And even a single reader telling me they enjoyed my comic is priceless to me, and it never gets old.

What can help this feeling of frustration is the community. I love the indie comic community. It feels both big and small at the same time. Now it's easier than ever to make and publish your own comic, but it's a struggle to keep doing it. These people are in the same community, and everybody's struggling, so everybody gets it. Some are doing better than others, but they've all been where you are now, or they will be in the future. There are certainly toxic people among the community, but in my experience it's a minority. You get the real sense that we're all in this together.

Comics will break your heart – not just once, but over and over if you stick with them, and in many different ways. But along the way you might find that you want to keep doing it anyway, because there's something special and unique about reading and making comics. Whether you're filling in those blanks between panels alongside a million readers or a hundred, you're all participants in that comic. Whether you're making the comic or reading it, that story is yours. When your comics colleague hits that Kickstarter goal, you celebrate right along with them. You puzzle out the way forward together with help from those who have been there before.

Comics might break your heart, but they also warm it in between breaks. This makes for a strong heart, and you're going to need it. Despair is inevitable but succumbing to it isn't.

Join us for the next issue."

--Joseph Duis, owner-operator of Heresy Studios, LLC

The Zombie Queen

She was once a trailer park resident and an abused prostitute
She was left for dead like a nobody, completely destitute
She then rose from the grave, seeking retribution
After an exploited life of pain, murder's her solution
She's the zombie queen and she can take on any form
After ending your life, your body's hers to perform
She possesses cadavers and unleashes an army of the undead
Her eyes change from full pupils to blankness and red
Full of glee and destruction, she has no mercy on the fools
She takes no prisoners, that's why she totally rules
From Elvis-impersonating pimps to truck driving werewolves
To a racist, southern cult to a chauvinistic, gamer boy
There was a sex-trafficking Santa Claus and an unfaithful husband
They all trembled in the wrath of Janey Belle
She took their lives and she sent them to hell
As she hitchhikes across these United States
Brutalizing the wicked and sealing their fates
She's the Zombie Tramp and she has one goal on her mind
Punishing the cruel world that left her behind

Last One Left

She's a South Side white girl, born and raised
The loud, passing train's unheard, leaving her unphased
She's got a Michelle Obama t-shirt and wears thrift store jeans
Yeah, she's a South Side white girl, if you know what that means

When she tells you about her 'hood, you best believe her every word
She's speaking out of love not fear (unlike those flighted birds)
She bumps Alkaline Trio and Eminem and quit smoking Camel lights
She's a homegrown Chicagoan who makes me feel alright

She's heard the endless, crashing waves as they collide into the lakefront
She smelled the gagging odors of the industrial park from a closed car window
She's walked down Michigan Avenue and felt the commotion of the city
As a South Side white girl, it's in her soul, and it guides her to her destiny

She slurs her speech and she prefers thin crust over deep dish
Working second shift makes her exhausted and striking gold's her only wish
Her uncle worked at the steel mill and her grandma was a maid
She's the first in her family to go to college, she dreams of getting paid

She knows she's got to duck when they say to duck down
She says she's the last one left since the rest left town
She stands out like a sparrow on a white dove flight
Yeah, she's a red-blooded south sider who makes me feel alright

Live Fast, Die Young?

There once was a time you believed you'd probably die young
Life was a waking dream with an early outcome
You pushed the limits of the rules and you flicked off the cops
You tagged the walls with a circle A, yelling "can't stop! Won't stop!"
You trespassed for no reason, it was just for shits and giggles
To relieve your anger, you pondered all of life's puzzles and riddles

You prayed to the moonlight every night for your suffering to end
The tangerine sky turned to black as you said goodbye to your dear friend
He left you behind on this earth to rot in isolation and cry
Exhaling joint hits out your nose in the vacant lot where you fly
The light of the moon was your only serenity in a life on the run
You were gonna live fast and die young in hedonistic fun

He was like your brother 'til the end or so you guys had said
But then he was left for dead, staining the carpet bloody red
You failed to have his back when he was stabbed to death
Without your brother by your side, you wondered what was left
You figured you would join him as it was you against the world
Be immortalized by a framed graffiti sketch or a boxcar mural

You felt alienated by established customs past down to you
Other than reckless behavior, what else could you do?

It made you feel rebellious, it made you feel so strong
The rhythm of your drum played instead of society's song
Like James Dean, you wanted to go out blasting
Or like Fred Hampton, you could be a martyr everlasting

But the years went by and your death never came
You passed age twenty-five, it was all so insane
Your prediction was wrong and you had to deal with it
Make something of yourself instead of living in shit
Leaving a young, good-looking corpse was a lost bet
With consequences catching up and expectations never met

Now you're in your mid-thirties and you just don't care
You just want to read a good book in a comfortable chair
It doesn't make you a sellout, it doesn't make you a pawn
It doesn't even mean you compromised or your fire is gone
It just means life rolled on and you must now adapt
But don't ever forget where you came from or the ideals you pack

Without Falter

Are we worth saving? I'm not so sure
Humanity's on a path where its destruction will occur
Climate change is an existential threat to the human race
And yet we all just coast along at the same dying pace
We never talk about it, never even care to mention it
It's always something else other than climate change
Are people really so stupid to believe it's a "Chinese hoax"?
And even if you do, why take the chance like a ghost?
Fucking chickenshit humanity will come home to roast
Do you really want to risk it? We'll all be toast
We'll die off like a beehive at the end of autumn
We're like a kid in the wintertime refusing to wear gloves
Getting frostbite like an idiot, ignoring what's above
As the ozone layer depletes and we don't even care
We're oblivious like a camper eaten by a bear
We're just a bunch of dipshits doing nothing to prevent it
Saying the scientists are "triggered" or throwing a fit
Doing nothing to stop it, doing nothing to drop it
Without falter, we just continue on like a rocket
So, I ask you again and the question brings me no glee
And for the record, I'm quoting the end of a movie
"Are we worth saving? You tell me"
I'm rooting for the zombies the next time I watch "Diary"

Death of All Life

Originally Published in "As the Moonlight Shines" by Nick Ulanowski

I inhaled the fumes of a damned civilization
Of a parasitic species hell-bent on destructive creation
Transcending all other life, we were superior like a God
Or so we proclaimed and continued on with our song
We lied to ourselves that this day would never come
But now with nowhere to run and no place to hide
Everything's come to end but at least I'm by your side

There were bombs and nukes, and smog pumped into the sky by the ton
And now never again will anyone feel the warmth of the sun
Never again will we bask in the light of the moon
Nevermore will we dream any dreams, only our doom
As I look up for the last time at the reddish orange sky
It just seems so fucking tragic like a tearless cry
The clouds begin to expand and collide, and yet, I have no need to ask why
Only kiss you goodbye as all life starts to die

Hold me close because this will be the last time you do
We won't ever again, it's such a shame but it's true
As the world begins to demolish and goes up in such pitiful flames
At least we're together on this dreadful, dying day
When everything once loved, feared or hated just fades away like a dream

Because it's the death of all life on this planet, this planet once green

("So it goes…")

Damned if You Do

Despair creates sadness, anger is when you expect more
It's a continuous cycle of disappointment, rage and mistrust
To break free from it would feel like such a release
This cycle of negative emotions and unfulfilled tribulations
It would be like removing a weight resting quietly on your chest
There would be no more fears, no more tears and no more toxic quests
But you don't ever halt this journey of negative emotions
Because if you did, you'd be left with emptiness
You'd be left with nothingness and nihilistic chaos
You'd be left with the ashes of former loves and passions
But most of all, you'd be left with apathy
Releasing the negative emotions makes you feel so numb
And what is numbness but a new kind of sadness?
So instead you hold onto the adversity and you persevere
You learn to adapt and live with the negativity
You need sadness to carry on
You control your anger and you minimalize your despair
You remain feeling real, you remain a functional person
You remain feeling like a human being with all of our flaws

Hope for the Cycle

I'm at the end of my journey, the story is done
Close the book, there's nowhere to run
There's nothing I can do, it's over like the sun
This path has darkened and the end has begun
The new tunnel I enter is full of questions
Speculation that haunts me like vanishing pensions
I don't know what I did, I don't know why this happened
I can try to look back but my peripheral has blackened
Unable to escape, I fall to my knees
Drowning in myself like the seven seas
Me and my lonely have nowhere to go
But only move forward into the new world I sew
I don't know how to move past this but one thing I know
I can make my reality how I want it even with this lost glow
It'll be okay, it'll be alright
The future can be bright with the past out of sight
The beginning to an end and an end to a beginning
The beginning brought end but the doorbell is still ringing
I will see the light, someday, some way
In between the pitch black and the dark shades of grey
No longer wander the earth with the questions astray
I will seize the day, someday, some way

Young Hoodlums

There's a mini mart by 211th Street that we used to walk to
As we'd talk about our lives and our hometown crew
Singing punk rock songs just to pass the time of day
Not letting the status quo get in our fucking way
We'd walk by abandoned buildings and pass the broken glass
Hailing from the south side meant we believed we were tough and crass

We joked how we were young hoodlums but really, we were just normal kids
Trying to figure out this crazy world in a system that was rigged
As the rich got richer, our neighborhood got more blighted
As they closed down all the industry, they called our area "white flighted"
While that was certainly true, there was something else so obvious
Company owners didn't care about us, they left our hood to rot in sloppiness

Some friends become your family and it's important to stay connected
That's why I stood by your side through thick and thin, never once neglected
Loyalty is a virtue that sometimes feels underrated
Everyone has their 15 minutes but then immediately is dated
In a world of trending hangtags and instant news, everyone is fickle
If I had a dollar for everything the public remembered, I wouldn't have a nickel

When we were young and stupid, we never would hold back
We were just a bunch of punks up against a deck that's stacked

We laughed through the good times and we partied through the tough times
Like, scrounging for change under the seats so we could pay a parking fine
We're like brothers from another mother with a bond that's never broken
And sometimes shared, spilled blood can create another connection left unspoken

Mic Drop

You were spending time with your kids, making sure they're smart and fed
Teaching them about the world, preparing them for life ahead
You wanted them to stay in school and told them it was cool
You said, "You don't want to end up like this guy, working in fast food"
You pointed to the cashier, and he felt it was kinda rude
"I have a bachelor's degree," he said, sticking up for himself
Teaching you a lesson about class consciousness and wealth

Only Livelihood

When I saw you across the hall arriving home from a long day of work
I had horror movies on repeat, feeling a lack of worth
My boss told me to blame Obama Care for my once full-time job becoming a part time
They couldn't afford to pay my benefits, like medicine used to treat humankind
They dialed back my hours like a robot they could toss aside when full of rust
I was like a worker ant being sacrificed for the colony I was told to trust

When I saw you across the hall, you told me you'd left your boyfriend
He left you several bruises you'll remember to the end
We smoked weed in your truck and we talked about our hopes and dreams
And about how everything in our lives had fallen apart, ripped from us at the seams
Even though time had run its course, we still were human beings

You said you were like Lori Meyers living in Unit 216 upstairs
In a condo by the train tracks, smelling of cooked, pumpkin seeds and cat hairs
To take care of your disabled grandma, you said a side hustle is a must
Charging men a subscription fee to see you thrust your bust
You got to pay the bills, you got to sell your time
All work under capitalism's the same, you said... relentless, cruel and unrefined

Our only livelihood's our labor, our only fans are our dependents
Everything is commodified, our bodies are bought and sold
We feed the bourgeoisie machine and we do as we're fucking told

The human spirit has a value, it’s about the price of 600 McChickens

Locked away in our cages and then lead to our slaughter

So you can tell your sons and daughters you were important,

loyal to the company ‘till the final hour

You said you were like Lori Meyers living down the hall upstairs

All proletarian labor’s the same, you said, we’re really just splitting hairs

Real Men

A real man doesn't drink tea
A real man doesn't drink iced coffee
A real man leaves out the cream and sugar
A real man drinks it black

A real man doesn't like a rom com
He only watches if his girlfriend makes him
A real man can't enjoy a slow song
A real man likes manly man things

A real man can't ever cry
A real man won't hug you goodbye
A real man will only shake your hand
A real man is stoic and bland

A real man doesn't wear his shorts too short
A real man doesn't wear all black
A real man doesn't dress like a rainbow
A unique expression is "metrosexual"

A real man doesn't have interesting hobbies
The only possible exception is sports
A real man stays on the grind

A real man gets laid and has no time

A real man has no self-awareness
If you make fun of these rules, he takes it literally
A real man doesn't understand the joke
Being an "alpha male" is serious business

These ideas about manhood are lost on me
It's too exhausting and I just don't care
Fuck your rules, I am who I am
I'll live how I want as my own man

Demons

It's a Saturday night and it's time to blow off steam
She's at the side entrance of the bar, euphoric it would seem
She's got on her favorite, plaid skirt with black fishnets underneath
And she's smiling so hard you can see her front and back teeth
She's yelling in excitement how the jukebox added her song
And smoking her last cigarette before telling everyone "so long"
She goes home to see her roommate passed out on the floor
She walks past this to her bedroom and shakily opens the door
Behind it all, she's terrified and doesn't know what to do
Her anxiety keeps on worsening because she doesn't have a clue
Her student loan balance keeps increasing each and every month
Her payments aren't enough to keep the number from going up
She's got a sink full of dishes and a pill bottle by her bed
She doesn't want to go to sleep where she can't stop seeing red
Memories of past trauma can't escape her so she has to drown it out
Using any distraction that she can instead of going down that route
She can't ever think too hard about it, she can't let it control her life
"I don't have it so bad," she tells herself, instead of reaching for the knife
She doesn't feel normal and yet she can't figure out how that can be
An idyllic and free-spirited, young woman is all that others see
"No one really knows me," she thinks to herself as she smashes into the pillow
"No one understands, all they see's a fraudulent glow"
She beats herself up and feels like a fake and phony
But everyone has demons to face by ourselves and our lonely

The Death Poem

To the tune of "The Death Song" by Marilyn Manson

You're on a bullet and you're headed straight to my heart
Even you're a scumbag too
I took a pill, ate your lies and believed you
You inspired my own art, it's true

I saw a singer beat an actress on the TV
Then I read they killed my hero too

I'll write a death poem, kids
Because it's all a filthy joke
I wanted to be just like you
I wanted to be just like you

I light up my novel on earth, this is hell
And pretend I never wrote it
Because I named a character after you
And now I know that nothing's true

I saw an actress kill a singer on the TV
And you know he was my hero too

I'll write a death poem, kids
Because all my heroes are dead

Brian, I'm not like you

Fuck you, I'm not like you

Fuck you, I'll never be you

MAGA Hat

With an Illustration by Kevin P. West

You wear your red, MAGA hat to the local, dive bar
If someone says they're offended, they can go back to their car
It's not your problem, you say, if they feel unwelcome
This is Trump's America not Marx's or Malcolm's
"All you snowflakes are the real bigots," you say
"Intolerant of my political views, it's not okay"
As the regular crowd gets thinner and the bar gets whiter
You say you're a customer here not a troublemaker or fighter
That's just how it goes because in America we're free
They're free to flee and you're free to be

Out of the shadows and into the crowd
You wear it proud and you say it loud:
"If the libs are triggered, that's their problem
If minorities are intimidated, it's because they're weak"
You're emboldened now and at your peak
The silent majority, you say, has your back
You feel like such a big man with your MAGA hat

You wear your red, MAGA hat to the family gathering
It's your grand nieces' birthday, so you sing:
"Happy birthday, young chum, and many more"
It's a festive occasion, this year she turns four

After downing your drinks, your smile turns to a frown
You scold your millennial nephew about the blacks and the browns
You ask him about his plans for the future and how he pays his bills
He says he has a medical card if he gets sick or needs pills
He lives on social security disability and he's voting for Sanders
He trusts Bernie to mean what he says unlike a politician who panders
You call him the n-word and you throw down your drink
"My taxes pay for your stuff just like those leeches with Link!"
He leaves sick to his stomach and can't believe he's related to you
Full of anger and sadness, he feels he didn't stand up or be true
When he arrived, he was happy to see everyone, but the night ended like this
And when he thinks back to that party, all he'll do now is get pissed

You've become such a big man with your MAGA hat
You tell it like it is about this and 'bout that
You were emboldened by the election of Donald Trump
The silent majority has your back, you say, like a fist bump
You wear it loud and you say it proud
Out of the shadows and into the crowd

KEEP
WHITE

The Path of the Righteous

You said that you meant well and you were just ending lies
when you outed your friend to your youth group, tearing up his insides
You said you loved the sinner but hated the sin
And wanted to end his temptation by washing his ailment within

You said you were righteous and you had God on your side
when you stood in front of Planned Parenthood, yelling at passerby's
You said it was murder and they had no right to choose
so you put a miscarriage on your sign, showing them what they'd lose

You said you were factual and not thinking with your feelings
when Israel dropped its bombs, leaving Palestinians screaming
You said it was logically justified and they had it coming
and the I.D.F should have more U.S funding

You say you follow this path because you've seen the light
You're completely convinced that you're moral and right
You say life is a test and you've done your very best
But have you ever considered you're failing like the rest?

Comply or Die

He didn't comply, that's why I shot him
I gave him a command and he refused
So, I capped him in his fucking ass
I yelled "get on the ground!" but it didn't last
He refused to do it and so I killed him
I murdered a man for disobeying my word
The bullets flew on camera, the whole world heard
The courts said my actions were justified
Fox News called me a hero and they called him a thug
Because this is my country, my city, my street that I run

Despotic Incident in the Park

He was fresh out of high school still in his teenage years
He was barely legal but had a full-grown beard
It was unshaven and unkept but he didn't mind
As he rode around town on his daily bike ride
He peddled down every street and explored the world around him
It was a fun way to get out the house and a healthy way to stay trim
Eventually he'd get tired and needed a place to rest
Relaxing at Fireman's Park, it was the very best
He'd sit under the pavilion at the picnic table
Or he'd pace back and forth, thinking how to write a tale

One day on his bike ride, he stopped by this suburban park
There was an event happening under the pavilion and on the grass
They were taking up most of the space where he came to relax
They were elementary school cheerleaders being taught by their couch
The young man paid them no mind, not really caring, but kept his distance
He didn't want to bother them in this public space meant for all
He dropped his bike on the ground in Fireman's parking lot
And lit up his cigarette, in his own world, minding his own business

His calmness was abruptly broken as a large, burly man approached
The kid felt like he was an animal being targeted and poached
The man asked him, "What are you doing?" loudly and aggressively

What did that even mean? Taking a break from his bike ride obviously?
He was young and naïve and didn't really know what to say
Just relaxing at a public park on this bright, warm, autumn day?
Instead he answered "Well, I'm over here because the kids are over there"
Thinking he was being asked why he was awkwardly on the parking lot's pavement
Instead of sitting comfortably on a park bench, that's what he thought he meant

The man had a look on his face this 18-year-old would never forget
He'd never been looked at this way before, much less by someone he just met
He was scum, he was unwanted, he was an American bug
to be vanquished and squashed like an incarcerated thug
The man whipped out his badge and yelled, "This is the police!"
He roared "Let me see your eyes!" – no justice, no peace
The young man leaned his head forward and let him take a look
He was loudly asked "What are you on?" as his bones shook
This teen had never been in a situation like this before
He was honest to a fault, confused and frightened to the core
He answered "caffeine pills" as if this was an authority to respect
Or like this plainclothes cop even cared about a NoDoz wreck
"Those are not caffeine pills!" yelled the cop, calling him a liar
Unable to tell the difference between a meth head and a kid a little wired
The cop said, "I don't want to see you around my girls ever again!
And I'll arrest you if you don't leave this park after I count to ten!"
The kid put out his smoke and quickly hopped on his bike
He peddled home to safety, away from cops and robbers and the like

It never even occurred to him he'd be accused of being a drug fiend or pedophile
This was a regular stop on the daily bike rides he'd been doing for a quite a while
He didn't even realize what the accusation was until he talked to his stepdad
who explained what had happened, making this kid just seething mad
This was his daily routine in his Monee, Illinois community
And we're supposed to have the right to be in the land of the free
"I shouldn't have left," he thought to himself years later, full of regret
"I should've put my hands behind my back and took the fucking bet"
He was doing nothing wrong and there'd be no illegal activity found
He could've made the cop look like a joke, handcuffing without grounds
In retrospect, he wondered if his developmental disability played a part
And if he used ordinary movements and speech patterns, this story wouldn't have a start

Don't be like this kid, please don't make his same mistake
If the police have you in their sights, they're not your friends for heaven's sake
You have the right to remain silent but if you don't, keep your answers short
If worse comes to worst and they arrest you, you can fight it in the court

Obstruction of View

You drove past a black man on the side of the road
Police were frisking his body and searching his car
You rolled down your window and yelled, "Fuck Monee cops!"
Then the flashing lights appeared, telling you to stop
They lectured you, asking if you hated this town or something
Then they gave you a ticket for air freshener - technically not nothing
They said it was "obstruction of view" of your rear-view mirror
You know those little air fresheners sold at gas stations? Oh no, oh dear!

Fuck You, Comicsgate

You wanted to celebrate the voices of women in horror
They called you a joke and they called you a bore
A women-only anthology? What a silly idea, they said
You had to prove them wrong, they left you seeing red
Motivated by spite and a need for smug satisfaction
To show them there was a demand, you had to take action
You did it yourself and self-published under your own imprint
With many contributors excited and responding to the calls you sent
You say representation matters but some call it "reverse discrimination"
As if America isn't rooted in being a sexist, white supremacist nation
Your horror comic anthology of all female creators was a success
But some people will never see the truth or at least not confess

They complain about "forced diversity" and "SJWs ruining comics"
They claim progressive politics cause sales to drop and it's simple economics
Any obvious examples that go against their narrative are dismissed
If you bring it up, they'll call you a "triggered libtard' and get pissed
They say they just want "storylines" that don't have any kind of "agenda"
As if literature and art haven't always had messages that just might offend ya
What they really mean is they don't want to see too many minorities or women
Or at least not new, unfamiliar ones, they demand only OGs not the kin
When something doesn't go their way, they'll hound creators online
Blowing up their mentions with bigoted insults, wasting everyone's time

If you're on the outside looking in, they can make all of us look bad
But they're just a small group of very loud, toxic fans, it really is sad

Fuck you, ComicsGate, and anyone else adjacent
Fuck you, ComicsGate, and anyone spreading hate
Fuck you ComicsGate, diversity's our strength
Fuck you, ComicsGate, go away, you're at least 30 years too late

Cease and Desist

Cease and desist letters are fun because I know you ain't doing shit
Cease and desist letters are fun, you bully-baby, entitled prick
Cease and desist letters are fun, so send me five or six
Just keep on sending them, wasting paper like a dick

You said you'd "escalate the matter" if I didn't delete my posts
But I deleted nothing and never heard from you again
You're not gonna sue me, it'd be a waste of time and money
Your goal is just to harass and frighten me, my god, you're fucking scummy

I'll post on social media what I want because every word is true
So, send me a cease and desist letter like there's anything you can do
If you take me to court for this, I'll have you laughed out of the room
Sorry I hurt your feelings, poor baby, you white-collar buffoon

You got a shoemaker at your law firm and claim you don't tolerate instigators
Manning torpedoes in Toledo and sending them to your client's haters
Was that a "cheeky reference"? Yeah, probably, just like how Bander snatched your idea
Your client's a fucking joke and a gaslighting sociopath with diarrhea

Cease and desist letters are fun, you embarrassment wasting your time
Cease and desist letters are fun, unlike your client's unwiped behind
Cease and desist letters are fun, so if you got some real beef
Tell him I don't eat red meat so PWNing him will be my treat

Null and Void

If you rant about how the system sucks
It's a-okay, we have free speech and thus
No one can really do anything to you
The FBI might question but no one will sue
We can start a revolution against the one percent
Without naming names, we yell and dissent
But if you take it one step too far
Folks can sue and you'll lose your car
They'll take your every penny earned
Repossess your house and burn down your fern
You'll lose your cats, they'll go to the pound
It'll be bad times just all around
That's why we must always be careful
With no specific names, keeping it null

At the AntiFa headquarters today
Loud and proud, I heard a fun guy say:
"I wanna shoot Jeff Bezos in the face
I wanna show him how some bullets taste
Come on, comrades, grab your gun
Load 'em up and shoot someone
Shoot Jeff Bezos in his face
To show him how a bullet tastes"

El Oh El, Jay Kay, Jay Kay
He didn't mean it that a way
For legal reasons, that's a joke
He was just playing, don't have a stroke
Stop making everything so damn serious
It'll start to make you delirious
Stop taking everything so literally
If you have a brain, then you can see
We're just playing, man, and yanking your chain
As you can clearly see if you are sane
I'm not responsible for what a crazed reader does
I'm just laughing off the rest of my buzz
The words I write aren't what I mean
What I really mean's an enigma unseen

I don't wanna shoot Musk in the face
Or show Elon how bullets taste
Come on, comrades, don't grab your gun
Don't load 'em up or shoot someone
Shoot the fucker's stupid face?
No! Don't show him how the bullets taste

For legal reasons, that's a joke
Lighten up, don't have a stroke
I don't wanna shoot Trump in the face
Or show him how these bullets taste

Em See You

We love Marvel, Marvel is the best
Bow down to Marvel, they're better than the rest
Bow down to Disney or we'll send you away
Send you to camps where you watch Marvel all day

We'll send you away like Jennifer Aniston
We'll send you away like Martin Scorsese
We'll send you away like that dude Marc Maron
You belong to Disney so come on and say it with me:

Marvel is the best
Marvel is the best
They're better than the rest
Marvel is the best

Starving Author

Another day, another night flew by
24 hours writing poems, getting high
Another day, another week had past
This starving author was built to last

Another time another week went by
I stood up, fist bared, and asked the world "Why?"
Each and every day I sat down to write
I was speaking my truth and living the fight

Another month, another year before
I worked low-wage jobs and couldn't take it anymore
Age twenty-one, twenty-two, twenty-three, twenty-four
I went back to school to become something more

Another year, another decade flew by
It seems so long ago until I realize:
Another day I sit back and write
And all the same demons are unleashed tonight

I was young and naïve but I still wasn't wrong
The system's still fucked, that's why I sing this song
I'm starved to write, I'll never stop

'Cuz speaking out is all I got

Another year, a lifetime goes by...
I'm gonna be a writer till the day that I die
Another year I'm rife with strife
I'm gonna write it down for the rest of my life

Our Struggle's Only Begun

You always knew something was missing
You felt deeply misplaced on the wrong side of the room
When they called your name, it felt like a dream
Something about you wasn't as it seemed
In the school cafeteria, they put boys on one side and girls on the other
They said you were a girl who wanted to sit with your brother
Today, you're awake and you feel so alive
You feel so free, you feel like you can thrive
As you yell to the world your truth no longer denied
You know who you are now and it's not what they told you
Your journey to the future has begun to mold you

Well, it turns out we're alive at twenty-five
Motherfucker, we made it, we fucking survived
But our story's not over, we still have so much to say
About American injustice and the world today

This wasn't how it was supposed to be
This wasn't the plan or what you agreed
It's like God played a cruel joke and He forced it on you
Infecting your body so it grows inside you
You took all the precautions you knew you were supposed to
Your man even told you he'd always take care of you

But nothing worked out so now you head to the clinic
You need it to end and you've made your decision
Your body and future are yours - not how others envision
At the front door, the protesters call you a killer and whore
But it's nothing you haven't heard before

Well, what do you know? We're alive at twenty-five
Motherfucker, we made it, I can't believe we survived
But your story's not over, in fact our struggle's only begun
And we won't be silenced or burned out by the sun

You got your associates degree in electrical technology
Now you work in a warehouse in the picking department
After a 12-hour shift, you come home, your legs sore as hell
It's like you're walking on knives or you fell down a well
If you work too slow, they say you aren't making rate
You must find and scan an item in four and a half minutes or less
Or else they write you up and call it "time off task"
You can't wear your headphones or listen to your podcast
It's boring, miserable work and in lonely solitude you must bask
You've been written up twice and a third will mean you get fired
So, it might be time to find work in another corporate empire

We're American bugs and life beat us down
But we're still fucking standing and we're all around

The story's not over, in fact, it's only just begun

We won't be squashed or burned out by the sun

American Bug

Sometimes I lay awake at night, pondering what he said
Staying restless and high-strung, I toss and turn in bed
He said, some read War and Peace and their takeaway is it's just a fun adventure
They'll consume media like buttery popcorn until they have to wear a denture
But others can read a candy wrapper and unlock the mysteries of the universe
They'll think about the bubblegum factory and ask how hell is any worse
What he said was true, there's degrees of depth in what we see
He was a wise man who went from rags to riches to infamy
His name was Lex Luthor and he said this in Superman: The Movie

Every morning at the office, I feel like a cog in the machine
It's like I'm in a swarm of locusts, faceless, and eyes on green
They say I can live the dream if I keep my head in the game
With a vision to invest, I can make it big, and every day won't feel the same
But in the meantime, I'm just a working bug without a name

When I get home from my long commute, I need to feel at ease
Zuckerberg needs me scrolling feeds, clicking ads and planting seeds
Netflix needs me paying fees, binging shows and posting these
I need to stay engaged so I can be a part of the conversation
If I don't watch the latest, hottest television, it'll be social ostracization
I won't know what to say, they'll remove me from the hive
I'll be isolated and alone, cast aside and eaten alive

When you speak to me of great literature, it's not something unknown
But sometimes I can't get past the second page before getting distracted by my phone
I understand your literary references, I read about it on Wikipedia
George Orwell warned us all about how The Party is misleading ya
And he coined the term "doublethink," that thing done by Donald Trump
And I know what Animal Farm's about, they explained it in the movie The Hunt
Snowball was an idealist pig, scorned and treated like the litter's runt
I know who Kurt Vonnegut is, and Ray Bradbury, so don't front
Don't call me an ignoramus, I read the headlines every day
I know the great authors' names and I know what the experts say
Fahrenheit 451 was about how censors burned a bunch of books
Like college campus "SJWs" or those Bush and Cheney crooks
I'm an educated American so bite your fucking tongue
These insults are getting tiresome you pretentious, lazy bum

When we reach the end, we want to feel like our existence mattered
When we're blowing in the wind and our ashes are all scattered
We want to feel like we accomplished something in the life we lived
We want to be able to tell our story proudly without them saying that we fibbed
Perhaps that's why some people never light the match and start a fire
They're too afraid of destruction to aim for the possibilities desired
The red, white and blue wants you to obey, conform and consume
But while you stay passive and afraid, a somber reality starts to bloom
You'll lose what makes you special, you'll lose what makes you you
If you let them get you, your proud story will never be true
You're worth more than your title or how the system's defining you

DO NOT

Acknowledgments

Thanks to everyone who backed *American Bug* on Kickstarter! This book wouldn't exist without you guys.

Joe Helm	Marimonica Murray	Julie Mueller
Four Corners Collectibles	Justin Anderson	Donna L. Ulanowski
Robert James Hultman	"Rhi Spawn"	Shawn Prior
Deidre Roberts	Daniel Clark	Ryan F. Skelly
Jason W. Gavin	Richard Pace	Ben Lacy
Howie Silver	Payette Art	Joseph W. Duis
Ann LaCorte	Schwmartz	Daybreak
Ben Grisanti	Juniper Waller	Lara Ulanowski
James Emmett	Mark Patron	Harris Grabarczyk
Steve Aultz	Kendra Reinshagen	Cora Linden
Rob Cavanagh	Jennifer	Lalinda De La Fuente
Tim Rossi	Claire Lourdes	Corey Hall
Eric Palicki	Destinee Jones	Arthur Crudup
Mika Exley	Michael Thomas Costello	Barbara Ann Siemens
Rick Rangel	"Jesus Christ"	Becky
Becky & Clyde Bagget	Grant Williams	Alex Finke
Ed Kolkebeck	Zone Comics & Games	Xiya Akande

Special thanks to my right-hand man **Jorge Santiago, Jr.** He not only drew *American Bug*'s cover artwork, but he designed the book's interiors as well. Jorge designed my novella, *Diesel Doctrine and the Temporarily Embarrassed Millionaires*. He drew and designed the cover to my first book of poetry, *As the Moonlight Shines* as well. Jorge is not only a great artist and a talented graphic designer, but he's been a great help. My journey of becoming the self-published author of three books isn't something I could've done without him.

Also, I'd like to thank **Richard Pace** and **Kevin P. West** for their interior illustrations in *American Bug*. Both artists helped bring my poems to life. Richard's amazing Jack Kirby illustration was sold as prints and played a significant role in the *American Bug* Kickstarter, too. Thanks to **Deirdre Roberts** for writing an excellent, well-spoken Foreword and for her longstanding moral and financial support of my writing. And thanks to **Joseph Duis** for writing a blurb on what it means for comics to break your heart, expanding on the meaning of my poem, "Comics Will Break Your Heart". This book wouldn't be the same without you guys and I'm glad I could count on all of you.

An extra special thanks to **Lindsay Moore** for reading a draft of the book, proofreading, and critiquing it. At least a handful of the poems in *American Bug* are better than they would've been without her input and suggestions. As an editor, Lindsay also played a crucial role in my novella, *Diesel Doctrine and the Temporarily Embarrassed Millionaires*. I am immensely grateful for her contributions. Thanks to **Ed Kolkebeck** and **Kristin Palmer** for signing books that were sent out to higher level backers of *American Bug*'s Kickstarter. Ed wrote the Introduction to *Doctrine and the Temporarily Embarrassed Millionaires* and Kristin drew a hauntingly beautiful, vampire illustration in my first book of poetry, *As the Moonlight Shines*.

Thanks to **Steve Aultz** as well. While he played very little of a direct role in the writing of the poems in this book, when I was a younger and a blooming poet, he guided and mentored me. He critiqued much of my earlier work and I'm a better poet because of him. And thanks to the comic book writers **Jimmy Palmiotti** and **Aubrey Sitterson** for plugging the *American Bug* Kickstarter to their tens of thousands of Twitter followers.

Finally, I'd like to thank the **Monee Police Department**, the law firms that sent me cease and desist letters, the convention that banned me, **Elon Musk**, **Donald Trump**, **Jeff Bezos** and #ComicsGate. All of you inspired me to give you a big ol' middle finger in the form of poetry. The great thing about being a writer or an artist is that we always get the last laugh. Always.

About the Author

Nick Ulanowski is a starving author and a local journalist who lives a few miles south of Chicago. When he isn't writing articles, he's reading comic books and critiquing movies online. "American Bug" is his third published book but it won't be his last. Be on the lookout for Nick Ulanowski the next time a news story breaks and a group of journalists exposed a corporate crime or government scandal.

www.ingramcontent.com/pod-product-compliance
Ingram Content Group UK Ltd.
Pitfield, Milton Keynes, MK11 3LW, UK
UKHW051126260726
13967UKWH00010B/2890

9 780578 251806